42 Lett

A Journey of Self-Discovery Through Cancer

El Roi, The God Who Sees Me

Michell Maxwell

"42 Letters to Myself: A Journey of Self-Discovery Through Cancer"

In the face of unimaginable pain and uncertainty, one woman's journey through cancer reveals the strength, faith, and resilience that she never knew she had. *42 Letters to Myself* is not just a story of survival, it's a profound and emotional testament to the power of self-discovery, the grace of God, and the unwavering love that carries us through even the darkest storms.

Written over ten years of struggle and healing, these intimate letters are a raw and vulnerable reflection of a woman battling cancer, fear, and self-identity. Through each letter, she finds hope, courage, and a deeper understanding of herself, and El Roi, The God Who Sees Me, who never abandoned her, even in the moments of deepest despair.

A journal of decades of my life. My own words. No editing.

Contents

El Roi, The God Who Sees Me

In the midst of the darkest days, when the pain seemed unbearable, when I could not find the strength to utter a single prayer, there was one truth that kept me from completely falling apart: *El Roi, the God who sees me.*

I didn't always understand what that meant. I didn't always feel seen. There were moments when I felt lost in the crowd, abandoned in my suffering, as if no one truly understood the depth of what I was going through. But God, in His infinite mercy and grace, reminded me time and time again that He was there. He saw me.

He saw the woman who was afraid of what the next day would bring, the woman whose body was ravaged by illness, the woman whose spirit had been broken, and yet still clung to hope. He saw me in my darkest moments, when I couldn't even look at myself in the mirror. He saw the tears that no one else noticed, my quiet cries in the night when I felt most alone.

And as I cried out in the silence of my suffering, God gently whispered to my heart:

"I see you. You are not invisible to Me. I know every part of you, the pain, the fear, the doubt. But I also see the strength you don't even recognize in yourself. I see the faith that remains, even when you can't see it. And I see the

beauty in your brokenness, the restoration I am bringing, even when you can't see how."

This truth became the anchor of my soul. It carried me through the nights when I couldn't sleep, through the days when I couldn't stop crying. It reminded me that I was never alone, even when I felt completely isolated. God was not distant; He was right there, in every moment of pain, offering His comfort, His love, His presence.

He sees you, too.

If you are reading this, know that He sees you in your pain, in your struggle, in your deepest heartache. There is no place you can go, no situation so dark, where His eyes cannot find you. He knows every fear, every tear, every thought you've had. *He sees you, and He loves you* with a love that never wavers.

If you've ever felt forgotten, unseen, or unloved, please hear this: You are not invisible to God.

You are cherished.

You are precious.

You are seen.

And no matter what you're facing, He will not turn away. He is with you, even in the places where you cannot feel Him. El Roi sees you, and He will carry you to the other side.

Let this truth fill your heart with peace.

Even in your darkest hour, you are held in the hands of the One who sees.

You Have a Purpose

There are no words that can fully capture the pain of fighting a battle that feels endless, the physical, emotional, and spiritual toll that cancer takes on a person. From 2005 to 2015, I lived through a decade that tested every ounce of my strength, faith, and resilience. It was a time of deep suffering, but also a time of profound revelation.

The letters that follow are my heart laid bare, raw, vulnerable, and deeply personal. They were written in the quietest moments of darkness, in the hours when I couldn't find the strength to speak to anyone else. I wrote them to myself, because at times, it felt like the only way to hold on. Each letter is a step in the process of grief, of surrender, of seeking God's presence in places where I could no longer see clearly.

But what I want you to know, dear reader, is this: none of the pain, none of the suffering, was in vain. It felt like a storm with no end, like a weight I couldn't bear, but through it, something beautiful was born. The God who walks with us in our pain does not waste our suffering. There is a purpose in it. There is a strength in it. There is growth in it that we cannot see at the moment, but will come to understand later.

I share these letters with you not just as a story of struggle, but as a testament to the love and grace of a

God who never left me. When I felt abandoned, He was there. When I couldn't find the words to pray, He interceded for me. When my heart broke repeatedly, He was piecing it back together. And He will do the same for you.

Whether you are in the middle of your battle or looking back on the scars that time has healed, there is something sacred in the act of vulnerability. In these pages, I have allowed my wounds to speak, not to wallow in the pain, but to remind you that pain does not have the final word. There is beauty in brokenness. There is healing in surrender.

If you are reading this and your heart aches as you journey through these words, know that you are not alone. I see you. I understand the depth of the questions, the weight of the grief. And I want you to know, with every letter, with every tear, God is with you. He weeps with you. He holds you. And He promises that He will restore what has been broken.

The title of this book is *El Roi, The God Who Sees Me*, and it is not just a title; it is a truth I hold in the deepest part of my being. El Roi means "The God Who Sees Me," and through the darkest moments of my journey, I learned this to be absolutely true. I realized that even when I felt invisible to the world, when I felt utterly alone, God was there. He saw me. He saw my pain. He saw my fear. He saw me in places where I could not see myself.

And His presence, His unshakable, unwavering presence, has been the one constant in a world that felt uncertain.

These words, these letters, are my way of reaching back to you in your darkest moments, to let you know that there is light. There is hope. There is restoration.

The road may be long. The pain may feel overwhelming. But I promise you this: it is not in vain. Every tear you cry, every moment of doubt, every setback, it all has meaning. God is using it to shape you, to refine you, to prepare you for a future more beautiful than you can imagine.

So, take a deep breath as you turn these pages. Let these words wash over you. Let them remind you that even in the deepest sorrow, there is always a way to rise again.

This journey is not easy. It is messy, it is hard, and at times, it feels like it will never end. But in every letter, I found one thing: the love of God is greater than any pain, and His grace is sufficient. Even when we cannot see it, He is there, loving us in our tears, in our brokenness, and in our fears.

This book is my gift to you. It is my hope that, as you read these letters, you will feel God's presence in the deepest parts of your soul. Let these words wash over you, comfort you, and remind you that even in the darkest places, His light is still shining.

And when you weep, when your heart breaks, know that you are crying out to the God who sees you, who understands you, and who will never, ever let you go. God sees you. He knows you. He loves you.

Letter 1
The Diagnosis

(April 12, 2005 - 1:30 p.m.)

"Be still and know that I am God." —*Psalm 46:10*

Dear Me,

Today, everything changed. One moment I was living my life, and the next, I was staring into the abyss of a future I no longer recognized. The doctor's words, "You have cancer", weren't just words. They were an earthquake, ripping through the foundation of everything I thought was secure. My heart stopped. My mind spun. I couldn't breathe.

Fear wrapped its cold hands around me, squeezing tighter with every heartbeat. Dreams I hadn't yet fulfilled, plans I hadn't even spoken aloud, everything felt so fragile, so far away now. My life was suddenly divided: before the diagnosis, and after.

I sat there in the sterile room, drowning in a sea of questions. *Why me? What now?* But no one answered. The silence was deafening. And yet, amid that silence, something broke through, a whisper, so soft yet so powerful: *Be still and know that I am God.*

I wanted to fight it, to push it away. Be still? How could I be still when everything inside me was screaming? How could I trust when all I felt was despair? But that whisper, God's whisper, didn't let go. It wrapped around my shattered heart and held on.

Tonight, I cried until I had nothing left. My pillow soaked with grief; my body exhausted from the weight of it all. But somehow, in the emptiness, there was a flicker of something else. Maybe it was strength. It was hope. Maybe it was faith, small, trembling, but alive.

I don't know how I'll face tomorrow, but I know this: I won't face it alone. Even in my fear, even in my pain, God is here. I will rise, even if I tremble. I will hold onto His hand, because when my strength is gone, His is just beginning.

With trembling hope,

Letter 2
The First Night Alone

(April 13, 2005 - 1:06 a.m.)

"The Lord is close to the brokenhearted and saves those who are crushed in spirit." —Psalm 34:18

Dear Me,

The house is so quiet tonight. Too quiet. It's the kind of silence that presses down on you, heavy and suffocating. The air feels thicker, the shadows longer, as if the very walls are mourning with me, holding this unbearable secret in their silent embrace. I lie here in the dark, staring at the ceiling, but it offers no answers. It only echoes the same haunting question over and over: Will I ever feel normal again?

The tears came without warning. I tried to be strong, tried to hold them back, but they poured out relentlessly. They washed over my face, soaking my pillow, each tear a release of all the fear, the confusion, the aching sadness I've tried so hard to suppress. In that moment, I felt like a child again, small, helpless, and utterly broken.

I thought the emptiness would consume me. But in that hollow, tear-soaked darkness, I felt something stir. It wasn't loud. It wasn't even clear. Just a quiet presence. A warmth. A gentle reassurance that I wasn't alone.

I remembered Psalm 34:18: The Lord is close to the brokenhearted. That's me, brokenhearted, crushed, shattered into pieces too small to recognize. Yet even under this crushing weight of despair, I felt Him there. Not with thunder or light, but with a stillness that wrapped around me like a fragile whisper, reminding me that I am seen and not forgotten.

Through the sobs, I whispered a prayer, not for healing. Not yet. That feels too big, too distant. Tonight, all I could ask for was peace. Just a moment of calm in this raging storm. And somehow, peace came. It wasn't overwhelming or lasting, but it was enough. Enough to breathe. Enough to hold on just a little longer.

Hold on, Me. You're stronger than you feel right now. Maybe you haven't seen it yet, but you will. And until then, you are not alone. You never have been.

Stay strong,

Letter 3
Telling the Family

(April 13, 2005 - 10:26 a.m.)

*"Come to me, all you who are weary and burdened,
and I will give you rest." —Matthew 11:28*

Dear Me,

Telling my mother and sisters was the hardest thing I've ever done. I can still see their faces, how their smiles faded the moment the words left my lips. "I have cancer." It hung in the air like a thunderclap, shattering the fragile calm. Mom's face crumbled first, her tears falling before she could even process it. She pulled me into her arms, holding me so tightly I could barely breathe, as if her love alone could fight the disease for me.

My sisters, my pillars of strength, stood frozen. Their eyes, wide with disbelief, filled with tears they tried to hold back but couldn't. Their silence spoke louder than any words. They were lost, scared, hurting just as much as I was. In that moment, my pain wasn't just mine anymore. It belonged to all of us.

I wanted to be strong. I wanted to tell them, "It's going to be okay," to offer some kind of hope. But my voice cracked under the weight of it all, and the words refused to come. So, we cried, deep, soul-crushing sobs. We clung to one another, our grief woven together, heavy and raw. But amidst the tears, I felt something else. A presence. A warmth. As if God Himself had wrapped His arms around us, cradling our broken hearts. I realized something profound in that shared pain: I don't have to carry this alone. I never did.

Jesus said, "Come to me, all you who are weary and burdened, and I will give you rest." Tonight, I did. I laid everything, my fears, sorrow, and helplessness, at His feet. And in the middle of the storm, I felt the slightest glimmer of peace. Not because the pain was gone, but because I knew I wasn't walking this road by myself.

Keep leaning on Him. You're not alone. You never have been, and you never will be.

With faith,

Letter 4
The First Surgery

(April 18, 2005 - 6:00 a.m.)

"Even though I walk through the darkest valley, I will fear no evil, for You are with me." —*Psalm 23:4*

Dear Me,

Today, it began. The first day of treatment. I stepped into that sterile room, my heart heavy with dread. Around me were others, silent warriors, each carrying their own invisible battle scars. There were no words exchanged, just quiet glances, each of us understanding the weight the other carried.

I watched the IV drip, each drop falling like a slow, steady reminder of time passing, time that now felt uncertain, fragile. The needle pierced my skin, and though it stung, the real pain went far deeper. It was in fear. Fear of what this treatment might take from me. Fear of what I would lose. Fear of who I might become.

I closed my eyes, trying to steady my breath, but my heart pounded relentlessly. My thoughts spiralled, drowning in the unknown. And then, amidst the chaos of my mind, I heard it: Even though I walk through the darkest valley, I will fear no evil, for You are with me.

Those words were like a whisper cutting through the noise, a gentle hand reaching out in the darkness. I clung to them with everything I had. God was here. Right here. In this room, in this pain, in this fear. He wasn't promising that it would be easy, that the valley wouldn't be dark. But He was promising that I wouldn't walk it alone.

One surgery down. Many more to go. But today, I made it. And tomorrow, I'll face what comes next, with Him beside me, every step of the way.

With courage,

Letter 5
Rediscovering My Identity

(May 14, 2005, 4:00 p.m.)

"But the Lord said to Samuel, 'Do not consider his appearance... The Lord looks at the heart.'"
—*1 Samuel 16:7*

Dear Me,

Eight hours. That's how long I was in surgery. Eight hours of darkness, silence, waiting. When I woke up, the room was quiet. No voices, no familiar faces, just me, lying there, feeling the weight of what had just happened. It wasn't the pain from the surgery that hit me first; it was the emptiness, the feeling that something had been taken from me, something I couldn't quite name.

I didn't lose my faith like so many others, but that didn't mean I felt whole. After two months in hospital care, there were days when I looked at myself in the mirror and saw a stranger looking back. My body

16

didn't feel like mine anymore. My health, my sense of normalcy, it all felt like it was slipping through my fingers, and I couldn't hold on.

But through the fog of loss, God was there, whispering truths I wasn't ready to hear at first. He reminded me that my identity isn't tied to what I've lost or how my body looks. It isn't tied to the scars or the battles that others can't see.

My identity lies in Him. In the strength He's given me to get through each day. In the faith that's carried me through every dark moment. God doesn't look at me and see brokenness. He sees my heart. He sees the resilience that's grown in the depths of my soul. He sees every tear I've cried, every fear I've faced, and He calls me whole.

I am more than what cancer has tried to take from me. I am more than what's visible or what's missing. I've learned to see myself through His eyes. And what He sees? He sees strength. He sees beauty. He sees a woman who didn't need outward scars to prove she's a fighter. So today, I look in the mirror, and I choose to see what He sees. I choose to believe that I am still whole, still loved, still me.

You are beautiful, even now. Especially now.

With strength,

Letter 6
A Night of Doubt

(May 28, 2005 - 1:07 a.m.)

"I do believe; help me overcome my unbelief!"
—Mark 9:24

Dear Me,

Tonight, the darkness felt heavier than usual. The quiet wasn't comforting, it was suffocating. Doubt crept in like a shadow I couldn't shake. The "what ifs" circled my mind, relentless and cruel. What if I don't make it? What if the treatments don't work? What if this fight is for nothing? The weight of those questions pressed down on me until it felt like I couldn't breathe.

I tried to pray, but the words wouldn't come. Everything felt hollow, distant, like God was too far away to hear me. I wanted to cry out, but even that felt useless. The fear, the uncertainty, it all seemed too big, too overwhelming.

And then, I remembered him. The desperate father in the Bible, pleading with Jesus to heal his son. His faith wasn't perfect. He was terrified, uncertain, but still, he cried out: "I do believe; help me overcome my unbelief!"

That's me. Standing in the middle of this storm, trying to believe but feeling the weight of my fear. I whispered those words tonight, through my tears. I believe, Lord. I'm trying. But I'm scared. Help me trust You in this storm.

I don't have all the answers, and maybe I never will. But I know the One who does. And tonight, even in my doubt, I'll hold on to Him. My faith isn't perfect, but it's real. And that's enough for now.

Keep holding on. Even when it feels like you can't, He's still holding you.

With hope,

Letter 7
A Glimpse of Light

(July 14, 2005 – 7:12 a.m.)

"The light shines in the darkness, and the darkness has not overcome it." —John 1:5

Dear Me,

I've cried oceans that no one sees. Tears so deep they've drowned my spirit more times than I can count. Every day feels like clawing out of a pit that grows deeper with each breath. I've known despair, held it, worn it, let it seep into my soul. And yet... here I am. Writing. Breathing. Fighting.

Today, something strange happened. I laughed. Not much, just a little, a hesitant, almost foreign sound that escaped my lips before I could stop it. It was real. The friend who made me laugh didn't know the war raging inside me, but they showed up anyway, armed with nothing but love. And for a flicker of time, the weight lifted.

It's been so long since I've seen light, I almost forgot what it feels like. But today, I remembered. I felt it in that moment, small and fleeting but powerful enough to pierce through the layers of my sorrow.

The darkness hasn't won. It's tiring. God knows it's tried. But here I stand, bruised, broken, yet unyielding. His light keeps finding me, even when I'm too lost to seek it. I saw it today in a friend's stubborn determination to bring me back to life. In their arms wrapping around my pain, refusing to let go. In the sunset that painted the sky with hope when I thought hope was gone.

These glimpses of light aren't accidents. They're whispers from God saying, "I'm still here." So, hold on. Even when it feels impossible, hold on. Because the light will always come. Maybe not in blinding brightness but in soft, tender flickers that remind you you're not alone.

You're stronger than you think. The darkness may linger, but it will never, ever overcome you.

With trembling hope and fierce gratitude,

Letter 8
The Pain I Can't Explain

(August 18, 2005 – 10:06 a.m.)

"My flesh and my heart may fail, but God is the strength of my heart and my portion forever."
—*Psalm 73:26*

Dear Me,

Today, I met a kind of pain words can't capture. It wasn't just in my body, though every nerve seemed to scream. It went deeper, wrapping around my soul, squeezing until I could barely breathe. It's the kind of pain that makes you wonder how much more you can endure, and today, I didn't have an answer.

I held onto myself, clutching my pillow like it was the only thing keeping me from unravelling. Sobs wracked my body, silent and loud all at once, echoing into the emptiness. "Why, God?" I whispered, my voice raw. "Why does it have to hurt this much?"

The silence that followed was deafening. No divine voice. No miraculous comfort. Just the sound of my own ragged breath and the relentless thud of my heart, proof that I was still here, even when I wished I wasn't. And in that aching quiet, something stirred. Not a solution. Not relief. Just a truth, quiet but steady: *My flesh and my heart may fail, but God is the strength of my heart.*

I realized at that moment that I didn't have to keep pretending I was strong. I didn't have to carry this alone. The cracks in my soul weren't signs of failure; they were spaces where His strength was seeping in. He was there, holding me when I couldn't hold myself.

It's okay to cry. It's okay to feel like you're breaking into a million jagged pieces. Because even in those shattered moments, you are not abandoned. You are not alone. You are held.

So let yourself feel. Let yourself grieve. Let yourself be human. And trust that when you can't stand, God will carry you.

With tenderness and unwavering hope,

Letter 9
Watching Others Live

(August 30, 2005 – 3:02 p.m.)

"Rejoice with those who rejoice; mourn with those who mourn." —Romans 12:15

Dear Me,

I sat by the window today, watching life move on without me. Children ran across the street, their laughter spilling into the air. Neighbors exchanged stories, their smiles wide and effortless. Families gathered, sharing moments that felt so distant from where I sat. The world outside seemed so alive, and I felt forgotten, left behind in this isolating shadow of sickness.

Anger bubbled beneath the surface. I wanted to scream, "Can't you see me? Don't you understand the weight I'm carrying?" But even as the frustration rose, something deeper overtook it, a raw ache, not because

24

they were living, but because I miss what it feels like to live.

Then, amidst the pain, a quiet thought whispered: Rejoice with those who rejoice. It felt impossible at first, but as I watched them, I wondered if healing could begin there, in sharing their joy, even from afar. Their laughter became a reminder that life, though distant, is still beautiful. I don't need to shut it out. I can let it seep into my heart, a flicker of warmth amidst the cold.

You'll get there. One day, you'll stand among them, not just watching but living. But for now, let their joy be a beacon in your darkness. Let it remind you that life is waiting, and when you're ready, it will welcome you back.

With patience and quiet hope,

Letter 10
When Hope Feels Fragile

(October 11, 2006 – 11:36 pm)

"We have this hope as an anchor for the soul, firm and secure." —Hebrews 6:19

Dear Me,

Tonight, hope feels as delicate as a whisper, a thread stretched so thin I fear it might snap. The weight of every pain, every unanswered question, presses down on me, and I'm terrified. If I let go, even for a second, will I fall into a darkness so deep there's no way out?

But then, I think of an anchor. It doesn't stop the storm. It doesn't calm the raging sea. Yet, it holds the ship steady amidst the chaos. That's what hope truly is, not a magic solution that makes the storm disappear, but the steady force that keeps me from drifting too far, even when the waves are relentless.

God is my anchor. When hope feels fragile, He is unshakable. His strength isn't dependent on mine, and I don't have to cling to my fragile courage because He's already holding me. He's always held me, even when I felt adrift or thought I was lost.

So tonight, let go of the need to be strong every second. Rest in the knowledge that you're anchored to something far greater than this storm. You're tethered to hope that will not break, no matter how fierce the winds may blow.

With quiet hope and steady faith,

Letter 11
The Loneliness of the Fight

(November 11, 2005 – 10:23 p.m.)

"Never will I leave you; never will I forsake you."
—Hebrews 13:5

Dear Me,

The loneliness is unbearable. People try, they visit, but when the door shuts, it's just me, facing this fight in silence. No matter how much they care, no one else can truly understand what it feels like to wake up every day and walk through this pain alone.

Tonight, the emptiness of the house felt like it was swallowing me whole. I lay in the dark, the weight of my solitude pressing down on my chest, suffocating. My heart felt like it was a million miles away from anyone who could understand. I closed my eyes, but there was no escape from the silence that screamed louder than any words. And the tears that no one had seen came again, the kind that come when you're so tired, so broken, you don't know how to keep going.

I whispered, "God, are You still here?" The words barely escaped my lips, but in the stillness, something shifted. It wasn't a voice or a sign. It was just... knowing. Knowing that in my loneliest, darkest moments, He is there. Not in the way I expected, not in a loud, undeniable way, but in that quiet reassurance that I am never truly alone.

Never will I leave you; never will I forsake you. Those words didn't take away the pain or end the loneliness, but they wrapped around my heart like a lifeline. In the depths of this battle, I felt something stronger than isolation: His presence. His love. Even when I can't see it or feel it fully, He's there.

You are not alone. Even in the darkest, loneliest places, He is with you. You might not always feel it, but He is holding you, right here, right now. And when it feels like the silence is too much, when you think no one cares, He is beside you.

With all the quiet tenderness of someone who understands,

Letter 12
The Mirror's Reflection

(January 4, 2006 – 11:00 a.m.)

"I praise You because I am fearfully and wonderfully made; Your works are wonderful; I know that full well." —Psalm 139:14

Dear Me,

Today, I stood in front of the mirror, staring at someone I hardly recognized. My skin was pale, my eyes hollow, and my body felt frail, as if it could barely hold me up. I tried to smile, but it was empty, a forced curve of my lips that didn't reach my heart. Who am I now? What happened to the person I once knew?

I turned away, unable to face that reflection any longer. The image of me felt like a stranger, a version of myself I didn't understand. But then, in the quiet of that moment, a whisper rose from deep within: You are fearfully and wonderfully made. Even now. Even in this broken, vulnerable state, God sees me. He sees the me beyond the sickness and pain, the me He created, the me He loves.

I took a shaky breath, summoned every ounce of strength I had left, and turned back to the mirror. This time, I looked past the physical toll of it all. I looked into my eyes, tired but still burning with life. I saw strength there. Courage. Not in the way my body looks, but in the fight within me, the fight that refuses to surrender. I saw someone who was still standing, even when everything else was crumbling. Someone who is loved beyond measure, beyond what they can even comprehend.

You are more than what the mirror shows. You are a creation of God's love, His masterpiece, no matter how broken you may feel. You are His beloved, and that truth will never, ever change.

With love,

Letter 13
When Anger Comes

(January 24, 2006 – 9:06 a.m.)

"In your anger do not sin; do not let the sun go down while you are still angry." —Ephesians 4:26

Dear Me,

Today, anger came like a flood, overwhelming and relentless. I was consumed by it: the unfairness of it all. The surgeries that don't seem to work. The pain that never lets up. The loss that keeps piling on. It felt like the world was so cruel, and I wanted to scream. To yell at God, at the world, at myself. Why me? Why this road, this endless struggle?

I clenched my fists, tried to hold it back, but the rage burned within me, hotter with every passing moment. It was a fire I couldn't put out. But then, in the midst of it all, I remembered: In your anger do not sin. It's okay to feel angry, but I can't let it consume me or turn me into someone I don't recognize.

So, I sat down, feeling every ounce of that frustration and pain, and poured it all out to God, every question, every cry for justice. And instead of turning away or rejecting me for my anger, He held me closer. He didn't need me to be perfect. He just needed me to be real.

God can handle my anger. He can handle the mess of my emotions. I don't have to keep pretending I'm okay. I don't have to bottle it up and suffer in silence. He's big enough for it. So tonight, I'm releasing it. I'm letting go of the anger and giving it to Him, trusting that somehow, even in this pain, He will make something good.

Breathe, Me. You don't have to carry this alone.

With release and peace,

Letter 14
A Small Victory

(June 26, 2006 – 2:11 p.m.)

"Do not despise these small beginnings, for the Lord rejoices to see the work begin." —Zechariah 4:10

Dear Me,

Today, I walked to the mailbox. It may seem like such a small, insignificant thing, but to me, it felt monumental. Every step was a struggle, every breath heavy with the weight of this journey. But I kept going, one foot in front of the other, until I reached that mailbox.

I stood there for a moment, letting the victory sink in. It wasn't a marathon; it wasn't a grand achievement, but it was my victory. And for the first time in a while, I could feel a glimmer of pride. I could feel God smiling with me, as if He were right there, celebrating alongside me. He reminded me that He rejoices in every small step, in every bit of progress, no matter how tiny it may seem.

These little victories matter. They are proof that I'm still here, still fighting, still moving forward. Each one is a sign of life, of hope, of progress in a battle I sometimes feel too weary to fight.

So today, I'm celebrating this moment. I'm taking pride in this victory, however small, because it's a reminder of how strong I truly am, even when I feel weak. You're stronger than you realize.

With pride and quiet joy,

Letter 15
The Power of Tears

(September 2, 2006 – 4:12 a.m.)

"You keep track of all my sorrows. You have collected all my tears in Your bottle." —Psalm 56:8

Dear Me,

The tears came again today, unrelenting and raw. They came like a flood, unstoppable, and I cried for everything, the life I once had, the life that now feels like a distant memory. I cried for the pain that never seems to leave, the endless ache that clings to me like a shadow. I cried for fear of what's still ahead, for the uncertainty, for the heaviness of it all.

My heart felt shattered, as if it couldn't bear another moment, another breath. My body trembled with exhaustion and weakness, and I felt so broken, so small, like I was disappearing into the darkness. I thought about the person I used to be, the version of myself that laughed without hesitation, dreamed without doubt, and moved through life unburdened. That person feels so far away now, like a fading photograph, and the ache of that loss brought more tears.

I was ashamed of my vulnerability, ashamed that I couldn't hold it together anymore. I wanted to be strong, to prove I could face this, but the weight was too much. In a moment of desperation, I begged God, pleaded with Him to take me away from this life, from this overwhelming pain. I just wanted to be free, to go home to Him, to find peace. The torment felt unbearable, and for a moment, I truly believed I couldn't fight anymore.

But then, in the middle of that storm, something shifted. A soft, quiet thought broke through the chaos: God collects every tear.

The words felt like a whisper in my soul, gentle and unshakable. And at that moment, something inside me paused. The tears didn't stop immediately, but I felt a stillness, a calm that gently wrapped itself around me like a warm blanket on a cold night. It was a peace I couldn't explain, a sense of being held in the quiet arms of a love that never let go.

The pain didn't disappear, but the ache softened, and I found myself breathing a little easier. Somehow, a tiny flicker of something other than sorrow stirred within me. It was faint, like the first light of dawn after a long night, but it was there. A small smile tugged at the corners of my lips, not because everything was better, but because I remembered I wasn't alone.

Each tear is precious to Him. Not one falls unnoticed. *These tears aren't a sign of weakness but a testament to the strength it takes to endure, to keep going, to face the unrelenting waves.* They reflect resilience forged in the fires of suffering. God sees every tear. He knows every heartache, every cry, every moment of fear. He collects them all, holding them close, never letting one go to waste.

So, cry, Me. Let the tears fall freely. They are not a sign that you're failing, but a prayer when words can't even begin to express the depth of your pain. God hears every single one, and in His deep compassion, He collects them, holds them tenderly, and holds you close.

As I wipe my face now, I promise myself this: I will keep going, even when it feels impossible. I will let the tears flow when needed, knowing they are seen and valued. I will trust that the God who collects them also carries me, even when I feel too weak to move.

With compassion, faith, and hope,

Letter 16
The Fear of Tomorrow

(November 14, 2006 – 3:16 a.m.)

"Therefore, do not worry about tomorrow, for tomorrow will worry about itself. Each day has enough trouble of its own." —Matthew 6:34

Dear Me,

This morning, the fear of tomorrow feels suffocating. It wraps around me like a heavy blanket, pressing down, stealing my breath. What if the news is bad? What if the treatment isn't working? What if all this pain is for nothing? My mind races with endless "what ifs," each heavier than the last, adding more weight to the burden I carry.

I can't seem to stop it. The knot in my chest feels tighter with every thought, like a vice gripping my heart. The uncertainty of what lies ahead feels like a tidal wave, threatening to pull me under. What will tomorrow bring? What if I'm not strong enough for what's to come? The questions echo in my mind, growing louder with every moment of silence.

I feel paralyzed by the unknown. Frozen in fear of what might be, I find myself bracing for an impact that hasn't even arrived. It's exhausting, carrying the weight of so many imagined outcomes. But then, in the midst of my spiralling thoughts, a quiet voice whispers through the noise: Do not worry about tomorrow.

The words are soft yet cut through the chaos with unexpected strength. They reach deep into the storm of my mind and still it, even if just for a moment. It feels as though they were placed there just for me, a gentle reminder to trust the One who holds my tomorrows.

He's asking me to let go, to loosen my grip on the fears that choke me and release the weight of what I cannot control. To stop running from shadows and instead focus on what is real, what is here, what is now.

Today, I breathed. Today, I fought. Today, I live. These are victories, no matter how small they may seem. And tomorrow, whatever it holds, He will be there too, walking beside me, carrying what I cannot, and lighting the path ahead.

So, let go of the fear, Me. You don't have to carry it anymore. You don't have to face tomorrow alone. Trust that His promise is enough: He will never leave you, not even for a moment. Today is enough.

With trust and a heart open to hope,

Letter 17
Missing the Old Me

(December 20, 2006 – 11:09 p.m.)

"See, I am doing a new thing! Now it springs up; do you not perceive it?" —Isaiah 43:19

Dear Me,

I miss who I used to be. The carefree laughter, the endless energy, the sense of invincibility that came with every new day. Cancer has stripped so much of that away, piece by piece, until I'm left with someone I barely recognize. I look in the mirror and don't see the person I once was. I miss the simplicity of life, when my biggest worry was what to wear or where to go, when the world seemed so much lighter.

But then, in the quiet moments, a truth settles in: God isn't done with me yet. He's doing something new, even when I can't fully see it. This pain, this struggle, the person I am becoming, though I can't understand it now, is shaping me into someone stronger, someone with more depth, someone who has learned how to lean on Him completely.

The road ahead is unknown, and the person I'm becoming is still unfolding, but I trust that I am being made into something beautiful. Though I may never be the old me, I'm beginning to understand that the new me is a version of myself crafted with purpose, grace, and love.

Trust the process, Me. You are becoming something unique.

With hope for what's ahead,

Letter 18
When Joy Feels Distant

(January 12, 2007 – 10:06 p.m.)

"The joy of the Lord is your strength."
—Nehemiah 8:10

Dear Me,

Joy feels so distant tonight, like something just out of reach, something I used to know but can no longer find. It's as if I'm grasping at air, desperately trying to hold onto something slipping through my fingers. I watch the laughter of others, and it stings. It feels so foreign, like I'm standing on the outside, looking in, wishing I could feel even a fraction of what they have. I wonder if I'll ever feel that kind of joy again.

I want to feel it. I want to laugh without the weight of pain in my chest, to smile without feeling like a mask I have to wear just to get through the day.

But then, in the midst of the ache, I hear a whisper: The joy of the Lord is your strength.

It doesn't come from perfect circumstances. It doesn't come from everything falling into place or from the absence of pain. This joy, the real joy, is the kind that comes from knowing I'm not alone in this. It's the quiet, unshakable joy of His presence, a joy that doesn't require everything to be okay but reminds me that He's with me, even when everything else feels broken.

Tonight, I'll search for that joy, not in the absence of my tears, but in the presence of God beside me. I'll look for it in the moments when He carries me when I can't carry myself, and when He whispers peace to my weary soul. And, just maybe, I'll find a little strength in it, a little hope.

I don't know if I'll ever fully grasp that joy again, but I know He will keep showing it to me in the places I least expect.

With quiet joy,

Letter 19
A Prayer in the Darkness

(November 11, 2009 – 3:24 a.m.)

"The light shines in the darkness, and the darkness has not overcome it." —John 1:5

Dear Me,

The night feels so much darker tonight. The silence is suffocating, and my thoughts are drowning me. Every minute drags on, and I'm consumed by a heaviness in my chest that makes it feel like I can't breathe. It's hard even to lift my head, and the weight of it all is too much to bear.

In the stillness, I whispered a prayer, barely audible, because it felt like my heart couldn't form the words loud enough. "God, are You still there?"

I waited, almost afraid to hear nothing in return, but then, like a flicker of hope in the deepest dark, I felt it, not a loud answer, not an explosion of light, but a gentle presence. A quiet assurance that His light still shines, even here, even now, in the midst of the darkness.

The darkness hasn't won. It can't win. His light is in every breath, every heartbeat, and even in every tear that falls in the quiet. He is with me. And though I can't always see it, I know He's here. He's holding me.

Keep praying, Me, even when the darkness feels overwhelming. Even when you can't find the words. Even when it feels like no one is listening. He hears you. He is always with you.

With faith in the night,

Letter 20
The Strength I Didn't Know I Had

(December 24, 2009 – 12:18 p.m.)

"I can do all things through Christ who strengthens me." —Philippians 4:13

Dear Me,

Today, I surprised myself. I got up, put on clothes, and somehow found the courage to walk outside. It wasn't far, but every step felt like running a marathon. Each movement felt like a battle I wasn't sure I could win. Yet here I am, still moving, still fighting, still somehow finding the strength to keep going.

There were so many moments when I wanted to give up. The weight of everything, the exhaustion, the fear... it all felt like too much. I wanted to crawl back into bed, pull the covers over my head, and forget that this fight was still happening. But then, a quiet strength rose from deep inside. It wasn't loud or obvious, but it was there, steadily holding me up, carrying me forward.

I realized then that it's not my strength carrying me. It's His. Christ's strength isn't flashy or dramatic; it's a quiet, unwavering power that shows up in the moments when I think I'm running on empty. His strength is always enough.

You're stronger than you realize, Me. Not because of anything you've done on your own, but because His power lives in you. Every step you take, no matter how small, is a victory. You're doing this. Keep walking, keep believing. You're capable of so much more than you know.

With renewed strength,

Letter 21
Facing the Mirror Again

(March 22, 2010 – 6:38 p.m.)

*"For we are God's masterpiece. He has created us
anew in Christ Jesus, so we can do the good things He
planned for us long ago." —Ephesians 2:10*

Dear Me,

Once again, I stood in front of the mirror today. The
reflection wasn't what it used to be. The scars are there
now, raw, jagged lines tracing the battles I've fought.
They're etched into my skin like an unspoken history,
permanent markers of everything I've endured. My
body feels unfamiliar, no longer just mine, but a
battleground. A place where pain, struggle, and
resilience collided, leaving behind evidence of the war.

I wanted to turn away, to avoid the sight of my own
suffering laid bare. But something held me there. It
was curiosity, defiance, or perhaps the faintest whisper

of grace. So, I stayed, letting my gaze linger on the reflection that felt so foreign.

In that moment, I reminded myself of what God says, **I am His masterpiece**. Even with the scars. Even with the weight changes. Even with the evidence of all I've been through. God still calls me beautiful, not for what the world sees, but for who I am. For the soul He created, the spirit that continues to rise even when it feels like it can't.

I am fearfully and wonderfully made. Those words echoed in my mind, clashing with my doubts. For a fleeting moment, I wondered: Does the Lord still love me despite these changes? The question lingered, heavy with insecurity.

It's hard to see beauty in what feels broken. But today, I tried. I traced the lines of my scars with my eyes, not with disgust but with a growing sense of awe. Though these scars may not seem beautiful, they are evidence of survival, resilience, and a fight that's far from over but hasn't defeated me yet.

I smiled at my reflection, not because everything was okay, it wasn't. Not because I had it all figured out, I didn't, but because I was still here. That alone is a miracle. Every scar tells a story, a story of pain, yes, but also of strength, endurance, and grace.

So today, I chose to look at my reflection not with shame, but with pride. Pride in the battles I've faced and the courage it takes to keep going. I'm here. I'm still standing. And for now, that is enough.

With self-love and quiet strength,

Letter 22
A Day of Gratitude

(April 18, 2010 – 4:32 a.m.)

"Give thanks in all circumstances; for this is God's will for you in Christ Jesus." —1 Thessalonians 5:18

Dear Me,

It's strange to feel grateful in the middle of this battle, but today, I did. In the midst of the pain, the exhaustion, and the endless thoughts that weigh me down, I found something to be thankful for.

It happened in a quiet moment, a rare pause in the chaos when I let myself truly see. The sunrise this morning painted the sky in colors I hadn't noticed in a long time, soft purples, gentle pinks, and glowing oranges, as if the universe was whispering a reminder: even the darkest night gives way to light.

I felt thankful for the small, beautiful things that often go unnoticed. The soothing sound of the wind outside my window. The warmth of the bed that cradled me when I felt too weak to move. The unexpected kindness of a friend who called, not for anything urgent but simply to remind me that I am seen, that I am loved.

I felt grateful for the strength to rise, even though every step felt like climbing a mountain. Gratitude doesn't erase the pain. It doesn't make it disappear or suddenly make everything okay. But it shines a light in the darkness, however faint, and reminds me that even in the hardest moments, there are blessings to be found.

These blessings are not always grand or loud. Sometimes they come in the quietest moments: the gentle embrace of a breeze, the sound of a loved one's voice, the soft warmth of sunlight on my face. Today, I found joy in those little things, moments of peace, small victories that whisper of hope.

And for that, I am thankful.

Today, I remembered another April 18, the day of my first surgery in 2005. That date is etched into my soul, a scar in time that carries its own story of pain, endurance, and growth. What a journey it has been.

So, keep looking for the blessings, Me. They are there, even now, even in the shadows. And in the searching, you will find the light.

With a thankful heart,

Letter 23
When Loneliness Feels Overwhelming

(June 22, 2010 – 11:14 a.m.)

"The Lord is close to the brokenhearted and saves those who are crushed in spirit." —Psalm 34:18

Dear Me,

This morning, the loneliness feels unbearable. It wraps around me like a heavy, suffocating blanket, pressing down on my spirit. I miss the easy rhythm of normal conversations, the kind where words flow without effort, where laughter bubbles up and fills the air, chasing away the shadows. I long for the warmth of another voice, the solace of someone who truly understands. But now, there's only silence.

The quiet is deafening. It amplifies the ache in my heart, a longing for connection so deep it feels like it might break me. I close my eyes and try to remember the sound of laughter, my laughter, but it feels so far away, like it belongs to someone else.

And yet, in the stillness, a truth stirs gently, like a whisper on the wind: "The Lord is close to the brokenhearted."

I pause and let the words sink in. He's here. Right here. In this heavy silence, in this unbearable loneliness, He sits with me. I can't see Him, can't reach out and touch Him, but I feel the faintest sense of His presence, like the warmth of sunlight breaking through clouds.

He doesn't demand that I be strong. He doesn't ask me to pretend the ache isn't real. Instead, He holds me in emptiness, His love filling the spaces where no human connection can reach. I feel Him in the quiet, in the moments when the tears come freely. He's there, catching every one.

I want you to remember this truth, even when it feels impossible to believe: You are not forgotten. You are deeply loved. In the moments when the loneliness screams the loudest, know that His voice is louder, calling you by name.

I may not have the laughter I crave or the arms of a friend to hold me, but I have Him. And somehow, that is enough. Even in this desolate place, His presence is a balm to my weary heart.

I don't know how long this season will last, but I know this: I am not alone. Neither are you. He is here, walking with us, carrying us when we cannot move.

So, breathe. Rest. Cry if you need to. But never forget, you are held, you are cherished, you are loved beyond measure. Even now, He is with you.

With comfort and quiet hope,

Letter 24
Learning to Trust Again

(June 28, 2010 – 11:26 p.m.)

"Trust in the Lord with all your heart and lean not on your own understanding." —Proverbs 3:5

Dear Me,

Trusting God has been hard lately. Every time I think I've surrendered my fears, another "why" creeps in, demanding answers I don't have. The weight of uncertainty is exhausting, and I've caught myself wondering if my faith is enough to withstand it.

But today, in the quiet, a thought stirred within me, a gentle reminder that trust isn't about having all the answers. It isn't about everything making sense or life feeling fair. Trust is about holding onto the unshakable truth of who He is, even when everything else feels fragile.

I don't need to understand it all to believe in His goodness. He has carried me through storms I thought I'd never survive before. He was there, steady and faithful, even when I doubted. And if He was faithful then, why would He stop now?

So today, I chose to trust. Not because it's easy or brave, but because I've seen His faithfulness written in my story again and again. I trust Him because I know His promises are true, even when my heart struggles to hold onto them.

It's okay to take it one day at a time. One small step of faith at a time. Trust doesn't have to look perfect, it doesn't have to be without hesitation or fear. It only needs to be real. And right now, in this moment, my trust is real.

I'm learning to lean into His grace, to let it fill the spaces where my doubts try to take root. I may not have all the answers, but I have Him, and that is enough.

With faith, imperfect but steadfast,

Letter 25
The Day I Felt Forgotten
(October 1, 2011 – 1:28 p.m.)

"Can a mother forget the baby at her breast and have no compassion on the child she has borne? Though she may forget, I will not forget you! See, I have engraved you on the palms of My hands."
—*Isaiah 49:15-16*

Dear Me,

Today, I felt forgotten. The world outside seemed to spin on without me, as though my existence had slipped unnoticed into the background. The phone didn't ring. The door didn't knock. It was just me, alone, with the relentless pain that refuses to ease and the silence that echoes louder than any noise.

I lay there, staring at the ceiling, the weight of loneliness pressing down on me. A question rose from somewhere deep within, raw and desperate: "God, do You even see me?" The tears came, unbidden and unstoppable, carving paths down my face as the ache in my chest felt too much to bear.

And then, like a light cutting through the darkness, I remembered: "I have engraved you on the palms of My hands."

His words, His promise, washed over me. He hasn't forgotten. He can't forget. *My name, my name, is written on His hands,* carved into His very being. It's not just a fleeting thought or a passing moment of attention. I am held, permanently, in His heart.

Even when the world feels distant, when the people I long for seem unaware of my pain, God is here. He hasn't moved on. He's not too busy or distracted. He is sitting with me in the silence, wrapping me in a love so steady and unshakable that it defies comprehension.

I may feel forgotten by the world, but I am not forgotten by Him. I am seen, truly seen, in all my brokenness, all my raw vulnerability. I am known, every hope, every fear, every tear. And above all, I am loved, deeply, fiercely, unconditionally.

So today, as the tears continue to fall, I will hold onto that truth. My heart may be breaking, but it is held in the hands of the One who will never let me go.

With a heart that's aching but still held,

Letter 26
When It Feels like Too Much

(November 3, 2011 – 11:00 a.m.)

"Come to Me, all you who are weary and burdened, and I will give you rest." —Matthew 11:28

Dear Me,

Today, it felt like too much. The weight of everything, the treatments, the pain that refuses to relent, the endless uncertainty, pressed down on me until I could barely breathe. It was as if the walls of my heart were caving in, trapping me in a darkness I couldn't escape.

I crumpled to the floor, sobbing, the words spilling out in a broken whisper: "I can't do this anymore." I felt empty and defeated, like every ounce of strength had been wrung out of me. I wanted to give up and let go of the fight that felt too big and heavy for me to bear. And then, in that raw, desperate moment, something shifted, not in my circumstances, but in my heart. A gentle voice seemed to break through the noise of my anguish, carrying words I desperately needed to hear: "Come to Me, all you who are weary and burdened, and I will give you rest."

Jesus wasn't asking me to muster more strength or pretend I was okay. He wasn't demanding resilience or bravery. Instead, He invited me, broken, exhausted, and afraid, to fall into His arms and rest.

So, I did. I let go of the relentless striving, the fight to hold it all together. I allowed the tears to flow freely, each one a silent prayer, releasing the pain I had tried so hard to carry alone. And in that surrender, I felt His presence, not erasing the burden but holding me beneath its weight. He is my rest. When the world feels overwhelming, when my strength is gone, He is the steady place where I can lay it all down.

I may not know what tomorrow holds, and the road ahead still feels daunting. But tonight, I am reminded that I don't have to walk it alone. He is here, walking with me, carrying me when I cannot take another step.

With a weary but trusting heart,

Letter 27
The Night I Screamed at God

(November 14, 2011 – 3:28 a.m.)

"I cried out to God for help; I cried out to God to hear me." —Psalm 77:1

Dear Me,

Tonight, I screamed at God. I didn't hold anything back. Every ounce of anger, fear, frustration, and heartbreak poured out in a torrent I couldn't control. The questions burst from me, sharp and relentless: "Why me? Why this? Why won't You fix it?" It felt like standing in the middle of a raging storm, my voice lost in the roar of the wind, but I couldn't stop.

For a moment, I thought I'd gone too far. My anger was too much. My questions were too raw, too unfiltered. But as the storm inside me quieted, I realized something I hadn't expected: God didn't leave. He didn't scold me for my anger or turn away in disappointment. Instead, He stayed.

He stayed, even as the weight of my words hung in the air. He listened, absorbing every tear, every cry, every whispered accusation. He didn't answer my questions, not in the way I wanted, but when the flood of my emotions finally ebbed and I sat there, exhausted and broken, I felt Him. Not with explanations or reasons, but with comfort.

It was a quiet, steady presence, wrapping around my shattered heart like a soft blanket against the cold. And in that moment, I understood something profound: it's okay to scream. It's okay to ask why. It's okay to let the storm inside me rage because God can handle it. He isn't fragile. He isn't put off by my anger or overwhelmed by my pain. He is strong enough to hold it all, to hold me, even when I feel like I'm falling apart.

So tonight, I'm reminded that being honest with Him isn't a sign of weak faith, it's a sign of trust. I can bring Him my rawest, messiest emotions, and He won't turn away. He won't love me any less.

Even in the storm, He is here. He hears me. He loves me. And when the screaming is done, He is the quiet that remains, steady and unshakable.

With raw honesty and a heart held close,

Letter 28
The Beauty in Brokenness

(January 12, 2013 – 7:48 p.m.)

"He heals the brokenhearted and binds up their wounds." —Psalm 147:3

Dear Me,

Today, I looked at my life; all I could see were broken pieces. Fragments of dreams that once felt so full of promise now lie scattered, plans undone, and the future a haze of uncertainty. I felt like a vase dropped from a great height, shattered into so many pieces that the thought of being whole again seemed impossible.

But as I sat there, staring at the mess, a quiet realization began to stir in my heart. God doesn't see the broken pieces as a lost cause. He doesn't sweep them up, brush them aside, and declare them useless. Instead, He kneels down with infinite care, picking up each shard and fragment and holding it as if it were precious.

And then, He begins to create.

I thought of how He works, how His hands, steady and loving, bind the brokenness together with grace and redemption. He doesn't erase the cracks or hide the scars. He transforms them. Each piece, no matter how sharp or jagged, becomes part of something new, something more beautiful than I could have imagined.

My brokenness isn't the end of the story. It's the raw material for a masterpiece only He can craft. The pieces I thought were too shattered and damaged ever to matter again are the ones He uses to reflect His glory.

It's not an easy process. The mending hurts, and the waiting is hard. But I'm learning that I can trust Him with the pieces. He sees the beauty in what I cannot yet understand. He sees the whole picture when all I can see is the mess.

So today, I choose hope. Not because I can see the final masterpiece, but because I trust the hands of the One who is shaping it. He's not done with me yet. And I believe, even in the ache, that He is making something beautiful.

With a heart learning to hope again,

Letter 29
The Day I Lost All Hope

(March 17, 2013 – 11:19 a.m.)

*"Yet this I call to mind and therefore I have hope:
Because of the Lord's great love we are not consumed,
for His compassions never fail. They are new every
morning; great is Your faithfulness."*
—*Lamentations 3:21-23*

Dear Me,

Today, hope slipped from my grasp. It felt like the last fragile thread finally gave way, leaving me adrift in a sea of exhaustion and despair. I lay there, staring at the ceiling, feeling like a hollow shell of the person I used to be.

My body is weary, worn down by the constant battle, and my spirit feels crushed under the weight of it all. For the first time, a thought whispered in the shadows of my mind: *Maybe it's better to stop fighting.*

Tears welled up, but instead of releasing them, I stayed silent, trapped in the emptiness. And then, just when I thought I couldn't feel anything at all, a memory surfaced, a small but powerful flicker of light breaking through the darkness.

I remembered a sunrise after one of my hardest nights. I hadn't expected it to mean much at the time, but it stopped me in my tracks. The way the light pierced through the heavy clouds, chasing away the shadows.

The way it painted the sky with colors I hadn't noticed in so long, gold, pink, orange, like a whispered promise from heaven itself.

That sunrise wasn't just beautiful; it was a lifeline. A quiet, unshakable reminder that His mercies are new every morning. Even now. Even in *this*.

I don't feel hope right now, and that's okay. Feelings are fleeting, but God's truth is constant. His love is greater than the depths of my despair. His compassion hasn't failed me, even when my own strength and hope have.

He's still here, holding me through the storm, whispering promises that will outlast the darkest night.

Tomorrow, a new mercy will rise with the sun. I may not know how to face it yet, but for now, I will hold onto this truth: God's faithfulness doesn't depend on my ability to hope. It's okay to be tired. It's okay to feel broken.

Just hold on. The dawn is coming.

With the tiniest flicker of hope,

Letter 30
When I Felt Forgotten by God

(July 24, 2013 – 4:28 a.m.)

"Never will I leave you; never will I forsake you."
—Hebrews 13:5

Dear Me,

I cried out to God today with everything I had, but all I heard in return was silence, the kind of silence that feels heavy, like it's pressing in from all sides. The waiting is unbearable, the stillness deafening. Over and over, I asked, *"Where are you, God? Why aren't You answering me?"*

The silence felt like abandonment, and for a moment, I let the doubt take over. I wondered if He had left me, if I was truly alone in this endless struggle. My heart ached with the weight of the questions and the emptiness that followed.

But then, like a faint echo breaking through the darkness, I remembered His promise: *Never will I leave you; never will I forsake you.* These words are etched into my heart, even when my feelings betray me.

Even in the silence, He is near. Even when I can't hear His voice, He hasn't walked away. Maybe He's not speaking in the ways I expect, but He is still here. I started to consider the ways He might be whispering to me, not with booming answers, but with the quiet assurance of His presence. The warmth of the sun on my face, the gentle rustle of the wind, the small mercies that still find their way into my life, they're reminders, faint yet faithful, that I am not abandoned.

His silence isn't rejection; it's an invitation to trust, even when I can't see the full picture.

It's hard, so hard, to believe when the waiting stretches endlessly. But I choose to hold onto this truth: I am held. Even in this quiet pain, even when I feel lost, He hasn't let go.

You are not abandoned. You are deeply loved, cherished beyond measure. Keep trusting, even when it hurts. He is closer than you know, and one day, you'll see how He's been working in the silence all along.

With a heart longing to believe,

Letter 31
The Pain of Watching Others Move On

(July 29, 2013 – 11:00 a.m.)

"Rejoice with those who rejoice; mourn with those who mourn." —Romans 12:15

Dear Me,

Today, I sat quietly on the sidelines, watching friends live their lives, laughing, celebrating, and moving forward with ease. It was beautiful to see their joy, but it cut deep. My heart ached with the sharp reminder of everything I feel like I've lost, of how stuck I am in this cycle of treatments, uncertainty, and waiting. Life seems to be speeding past me while I struggle just to hold on.

It's hard to rejoice when your own heart feels heavy and broken. The weight of longing, for what once was or what could have been, presses harder in moments

72

like these. I've wrestled with guilt for feeling this way, for not being able to fully share in their happiness.

But maybe, just maybe, I don't have to pretend. God doesn't ask me to deny my pain or hide my tears behind a mask of forced smiles. He invites me to be honest, to mourn when I need to, to feel the ache and acknowledge the loss. It's okay to recognize the gap between where I am and where I want to be.

At the same time, He gently reminds me that the joy I see in others isn't meant to hurt me, it's a whisper of hope. A quiet assurance that life continues, even in the shadow of my pain. Their joy doesn't make my struggles any less real, and my pain doesn't cancel their happiness. Both can coexist.

So, cry if you need to. Let the tears fall. Let the ache rise. Mourn the life you miss and the plans that feel out of reach. But don't forget this: joy hasn't forgotten you. Even in this season of heartache, it's waiting. It may feel far away now, but it will find you again.

Until that day comes, let the laughter of others remind you that light still exists, and that one day, you'll feel it warming your heart again.

With aching honesty and quiet hope,

Letter 32
The Strength of Tears

(August 8, 2013 – 3:21 a.m.)

"Those who sow with tears will reap with songs of joy." —Psalm 126:5

Dear Me,

I cried again today. Not the quiet, gentle tears that slip down unnoticed, but the kind of sobbing that leaves your chest heaving, your throat raw, and your body trembling. It felt like the tears were pulling something out of me, draining the last reserves of strength I thought I had. I felt hollow, empty, and so exhausted.

But as the sobs quieted, another thought emerged: tears aren't the enemy. They're not a sign of weakness or defeat. Perhaps they are seeds, planted deep in the soil of my soul, watered by pain but destined to bring forth something beautiful in time.

God sees every tear, even the ones I think no one notices. He doesn't dismiss them or brush them aside. Each one is precious to Him, a testament to the depth of this journey and the weight of my heart. He collects them, treasures them, and promises something extraordinary: *those who sow in tears will reap songs of joy.*

It's hard to believe that right now. Joy feels so distant, almost like a forgotten memory. But God's promises don't depend on how I feel at this moment. They are real, unchanging, and steady, even when my emotions aren't aligned.

So cry, dear self. Let the tears fall as they need to. They aren't wasted; they're doing a quiet, sacred work within you. They are a language of faith when words fail, a way of saying, *I don't understand, but I trust You, God.*

One day, the seeds of these tears will bloom into something unexpected and beautiful. Maybe not today or tomorrow, but joy will come. Until then, let yourself grieve, knowing that even in your emptiness, you are being held by a love that never let go.

With tenderness and hope,

Letter 33
The Night I Couldn't Breathe

(June 11, 2014 – 2:03 a.m.)

"The Lord is my shepherd; I shall not want. He makes me lie down in green pastures. He leads me beside still waters. He restores my soul." —Psalm 23:1-3

Dear Me,

Tonight, it felt like my soul couldn't catch its breath. The weight of everything, fear, exhaustion, loneliness, pressed down so heavily that it seemed impossible to stand, let alone move forward. My hands trembled as I clutched the pillow, desperate to stifle the sobs threatening to shatter what little strength I had left.

In the darkness, I whispered, "God, help me." It felt like a plea lost in the void, unanswered and unheard. The silence that followed was deafening, and for a moment, I wondered if I was truly alone.

But then, out of nowhere, a memory surfaced, a tender, distant echo from my childhood. I remembered my mother humming Psalm 23 as she tucked me into bed. Her voice, steady and full of love, wove its way into my heart, carrying a promise of safety even when the world around me felt overwhelming. I could almost feel her hands smoothing my hair, her presence reminding me that I was seen, loved, and held.

That same Shepherd she sang about is here with me now. He hasn't left, even in the moments when the darkness feels impenetrable. He's here, gently guiding me, leading me beside still waters, even when I feel like I'm drowning. He's restoring me, not in dramatic, sweeping gestures, but breath by breath, tear by tear. I don't know how I'll make it through tonight, but I'll trust Him to carry me. Not because I feel strong or full of faith, but because He is faithful, even when I'm not.

So let the tears fall. Let them wash over you and know that each one is seen. Let the Shepherd hold you in the way only He can, wrapping you in His love and grace. You are not alone, not tonight, not ever.

With a trembling heart and a flicker of trust,

Letter 34
The Day I Wanted to Give Up

(August 11, 2015 – 1:19 p.m.)

"Even though I walk through the darkest valley, I will fear no evil, for You are with me." —Psalm 23:4

Dear Me,

Today, I found myself standing on the edge of despair, staring into an endless and unrelenting void. I felt the weight of everything pressing down on me, the exhaustion of fighting, the ache of hope slipping away, the relentless struggle that left me questioning if I had anything left to give. I was tired. Tired of pretending I was okay when every part of me was breaking. The valley felt too dark, the walls too steep, and I couldn't see a way out.

I wanted to let go, to give in to the silence and stillness, to stop carrying the unbearable weight. But in that moment of surrender, when I thought I had nothing left, a steady whisper broke through: *You are not walking alone.*

God hasn't left me in this valley, no matter how lost or forgotten I feel. He's here, walking beside me, even in the shadows and the silence. I can't always feel Him, but I know He's there, holding my hand and guiding me, step by step. It's not about seeing the entire path; it's about trusting the One who lights the way, even if it's just enough for the next step.

So, I won't give up, not today. I'll hold on, even if it's just by a thread. I'll hold on to His promise: that I am not abandoned, that His strength is made perfect in my weakness, and that this valley, no matter how deep or dark, is not my forever.

Dear self, keep going. Even in the darkest valley, His light is soft, steady, and unshakable. Cling to it. Cling to Him.

With every ounce of strength I have left,

Letter 35
The Ache of Remembering

(August 16, 2015 – 2:48 p.m.)

"He will wipe every tear from their eyes. There will be no more death or mourning or crying or pain, for the old order of things has passed away."
—Revelation 21:4

Dear Me,

Today, I pulled out the old photo albums, and with each page turned, my heart grew heavier. Every image was a snapshot of a life I hardly recognize now, a life full of laughter, carefree dreams, and plans untouched by the shadow of this fight. Each photo seemed to whisper of a version of me I deeply miss, a life that feels impossibly far away.

I traced the faces in the pictures, lingering on moments that once brought so much joy. But today, they felt like a painful reminder of what's been lost. I wept, not just for the memories, but for the loss of who

I thought I'd be. It felt as if the weight of everything I've endured came rushing to the surface, leaving me raw and aching.

And yet, even in that flood of grief, a quiet truth settled in my spirit: *This is not the end*. The pain I carry, the dreams that feel shattered, the plans that have fallen apart, they don't get the final say. God promises that one day, every tear will be wiped away. Every fragment of brokenness will be made whole in ways I can't yet imagine.

Until that day, it's okay to mourn. It's okay to let the ache linger. Because that ache is a testament to the beauty of what was, a life lived, love shared, memories made. And as much as it hurts, it's also a reminder that hope remains. Even now, even here, hope still whispers that there's more to this story.

So let the tears fall. Let yourself remember. And as you hold onto those precious pieces of the past, know this: God is holding onto you.

With love for what was and hope for what will be,

Letter 36
The Moment I Wanted to Walk away

(September 4, 2015 – 12:34 p.m.)

"My God, my God, why have You forsaken me?"
—Matthew 27:46

Dear Me,

Today, the emptiness swallowed me whole. The pain clawed at every corner of my heart, and the silence felt like a wall too thick to break through. I cried out, "God, where are You?" My voice trembled, filled with desperation, but no answer came. The stillness was deafening. In that moment, I felt utterly forgotten, like I had been left alone to carry a burden far too heavy for one soul to bear.

The loneliness was overwhelming, and I couldn't shake the thought that I had been abandoned. But then, a memory surfaced, Jesus on the cross, in His darkest hour, crying out with a voice so human, so full of anguish: *"My God, My God, why have You forsaken Me?"* Even He, the Son of God, knew what it was like to feel the weight of abandonment. He felt the crushing silence, the piercing loneliness.

Yet in His pain, He didn't let go of His trust in God. Even when He couldn't feel His Father's presence, He surrendered His spirit into His hands. That kind of trust, born in the darkest of valleys, reminds me that my feelings don't dictate God's presence. He is here, even when the silence feels unbearable.

I may not hear Him today. I may not feel Him wrapping His arms around me in the way I long for. But I know He is with me. He hasn't left, even in the quiet. He hasn't forgotten me. He is carrying me, even when I feel forsaken.

Hold on, dear self. Trust that even when you feel alone, you are never truly abandoned. The God who held Jesus through His darkest hour is holding you now.

With aching but steadfast faith,

Letter 37
The Pain of Watching My Body Change

(October 22, 2015 – 6:42 p.m.)

"For we live by faith, not by sight."
—2 Corinthians 5:7

Dear Me,

I stood in front of the mirror today, and for a long moment, I didn't recognize the person looking back at me. The reflection seemed so distant, so foreign. My body is different, frailer, weaker. The face I once knew is now etched with the marks of battles fought; the skin altered in ways I never imagined. I barely recognize who I've become, and it breaks my heart.

I want to shout at my reflection, demand answers, and scream at the unfairness of it all. But instead, all I can do is cry. I miss the woman I was before this fight began, the woman who felt strong, beautiful, whole. I miss the me who could move through life without fear, without pain.

But in this heartache, something is shifting within me. I am learning that my worth was never in my body. It was never in how I looked, my strength, or how others saw me. It was never in the things that the world tells me should define me. My worth is found in the love God has for me, in the life He's given me, no matter how broken or altered it may seem.

I may not look like who I once was, and I may not feel like the woman I remember, but I am still me. I am still precious in His sight, still deeply loved, still worthy in His eyes.

Even when the tears make it hard to see, even when the changes feel too much to bear, remember this: You are more than what you can see in the mirror. Your reflection doesn't determine your worth; it is defined by the love of the One who created you and calls you His own.

With a heart that's broken but grateful,

Letter 38
The Day I Couldn't Pray

(November 11, 2015 - 2:14 a.m.)

"The Spirit helps us in our weakness. We do not know what we ought to pray for, but the Spirit himself intercedes for us through wordless groans."
—Romans 8:26

Dear Me,

There was a day, not too long ago, when I couldn't find the words to pray. Every prayer felt stuck inside, caught in the tangled mess of grief, fear, and confusion. I tried to open my mouth, to speak to God, but nothing came. My heart was too heavy, my mind too clouded to even know where to begin.

And in the midst of that silence, I remembered something beautiful, something that offered a shred of comfort: *The Spirit helps us in our weakness.* When we can't find the words, He speaks for us. When our hearts are too broken to form sentences, He groans with us. Even in the silence, when I couldn't pray, God was still hearing my heart.

If you can't pray today, that's okay. You don't need the right words or the strength to speak. The Spirit is praying for you. He's holding your pain, your silence, your unspoken thoughts. Even when you feel too weak to pray, He's carrying your burdens with you.

You're not alone in this. God is with you, even in your silence.

With a heart too tired to speak,

Letter 39
The Moment I Almost Let Go

(November 23, 2015 – 10:11 p.m.)

"But He said to me, 'My grace is sufficient for you, for My power is made perfect in weakness.'"
—2 Corinthians 12:9

Dear Me,

I was so close today. So close to giving up, to letting the weight of it all crush me. I wanted to say, *"I can't do this anymore."* The pain, the fear of what lies ahead, it all felt like too much. I thought about surrendering, but not to God. I wanted to surrender to the darkness, to let it swallow me whole.

But then, in that moment of utter exhaustion, I heard a whisper deep within my soul. It was softer than a breath, yet stronger than anything I'd felt before: *My grace is sufficient for you.* And in that fragile whisper, I found a flicker of strength, just enough to take one more breath, to keep going for one more moment.

I don't have all the strength I need, but He does. And when I feel like I have nothing left to give, I can trust that His grace will always be enough to carry me through.

With a heart still bruised but still holding on,

Letter 40
The Fear That Won't Leave Me

(November 28, 2015 – 1:14 a.m.)

"Do not fear, for I have redeemed you; I have summoned you by name; you are mine." —Isaiah 43:1

Dear Me,

Fear doesn't let go. It lingers in the quiet moments, whispering, *What if it gets worse? What if you don't make it?* It's there in every scan, every appointment, every sleepless night, a shadow that never fully fades, no matter how much I pray for it to leave.

But then I remember something that silences that fear: *I have redeemed you; I have summoned you by name; you are mine.* In the face of every fear, God calls me by name. I am His. And if I am His, nothing can truly harm me. The fear may still linger, but I am never alone.

It may never fully go away, but His love is greater than anything fear can bring. His love is the shield that guards my heart, the strength that carries me forward.

With trembling courage,

Letter 41
The Moment I Realized God Was My Only Hope

(December 19, 2015 – 5:46 a.m.)

"We are hard pressed on every side, but not crushed; perplexed, but not in despair; persecuted, but not abandoned; struck down, but not destroyed."
—2 Corinthians 4:8-9

Dear Me,

There was a moment, just a moment, though it felt like eternity, when I realized that all I had left was God. Everything else felt uncertain, fragile. The treatments weren't a guarantee. The people I loved couldn't carry me forever. The world seemed to keep moving while I stood frozen in place. It was just me and Him.

In that moment of raw, empty honesty, I asked myself: *What happens when all you have left is God?* And the answer broke me wide open, *God is enough.*

I felt the weight of my helplessness, the aching reminder that I cannot do this on my own. But I also felt the overwhelming truth: I don't have to. He is enough. He is my strength when mine is gone. He is my hope when everything feels hopeless. He is my breath when I can't breathe.

I will cry, and I will hurt, and I will fear, but in the end, the God who holds my tears will never let me go. In Him, I am not crushed. I am not abandoned. Even when I'm broken, I am not destroyed.

And as the tears fall, I know that God is here. He is enough. Always.

With a heart shattered and yet held,

Letter 42
When I Said Goodbye

(December 27, 2015 – 2:18 p.m.)

"So do not fear, for I am with you; do not be dismayed, for I am your God. I will strengthen you and help you; I will uphold you with my righteous right hand." —Isaiah 41:10

Dear Self,

This is the letter I never thought I'd write. The moment that still echoes like a silent scream through the corridors of my soul.

The moment I said goodbye.

I remember it vividly: The sterile air of the hospital, the sound of beeping machines slowing into a rhythm of finality, and the helpless ache in my chest as I watched the light in their eyes flicker one last time. You didn't just lose someone that day, you lost a part of yourself. The part that believed love could hold back death, the part that thought prayers always meant preservation, not peace.

The part that clung so tightly it forgot that letting go could also be holy. At 2:18 p.m., the world didn't stop spinning. But yours did, the sun still shone, but everything looked dimmer. People still spoke, but your ears could only hear the echo of loss.

And your hands…oh, your trembling hands, held a silence that once held life. But let me tell you something, sweetheart: That goodbye was not the end. It was a turning point. Because in your breaking, God began building.

He caught every tear you couldn't wipe away.

He held you up when you collapsed into yourself.

He whispered truth into the void left by death: "You are not alone."

You didn't know it then, but that goodbye became the birthplace of your becoming. In loss, you found purpose. In emptiness, you discovered depth. In silence, you heard the voice of the One who never leaves.

I know you wanted one more moment. One more word. One more laugh.

But God gave you something else. A promise.

That He would strengthen you.

Help you.

Uphold you.

And He did. That was the day you laid down your gloves. Stopped trying to fix what only Heaven could heal. That was the day you wept like a child and God held you like a Father.

Now look at you 😊

Still standing.

Still breathing.

Still believing.

You have survived every wave that tried to drown you. And now, your story, this story, is light for someone else's dark. Your goodbye gave birth to this letter. And this letter is the proof that grief does not have the final word. Grace does.

With all my heart,

Your Future Self

Still healing, still rising, still loved.

Closing

As I close the final page of this journey, I find myself filled with a bittersweet sense of peace, peace that only comes after walking through the storm and emerging on the other side.

Not unscathed, but stronger. More whole. There were days I didn't think I could go on, when the pain was so overwhelming, I couldn't see beyond it. But I kept moving forward, step by step, trusting that even in the moments I couldn't feel His presence, God was still with me.

And so, here I stand, changed, scarred, and yet, somehow, more whole than I ever thought possible. These letters have been my sanctuary, my refuge. And I offer them to you now. They were written for me, but I believe they were meant for you too. For you, who are walking through your own storm, fighting your own battles, wondering if you can hold on just a little longer?

To you, I say, *you are not alone.* The pain, the heartache, the fear, they are real. But so is the love of a God who will never let you go. His grace will sustain you, even when you feel like you're falling apart. There is beauty in your brokenness and healing waiting on the other side of your tears.

This is not the end of the story, but the beginning of something new. A story of hope, renewal, and strength that can only be found in surrender. Your journey is yours alone, but know this: you do not walk it in vain. Every tear, every moment of doubt, every setback, it all has meaning. God is using it to shape, refine, and prepare you for a future more beautiful than you can imagine.

So, as you turn the page, know this: You are loved. You are seen. And you are worthy of all the healing and grace that awaits you. I've walked through the valley and come out on the other side. And I promise you, so will you. There is nothing that will break you beyond repair. Nothing is too dark, too broken, or too far gone for His redemption.

With Love,

—*Michell*

Made in the USA
Middletown, DE
17 July 2025